Pre-Reading Book of Pop

Popular Christmas • Popular Hits • Popular Praise

32 Arrangements for Beginning Pianists
With Optional Teacher/Parent Accompaniments

Produced by
Alfred Music Publishing Co., Inc.
P.O. Box 10003
Van Nuys, CA 91410-0003
alfred.com

Printed in USA.

ISBN-10: 0-7390-8661-8
ISBN-13: 978-0-7390-8661-2

Cover Illustrations
Photo film and video icons: © istockphoto / kathykonkle • Playful children, kids mid-air jumping, children showing talents: © istockphoto / 4x6 •
Christmas preparation: © istockphoto / AdrianHillman • Stringed Instruments: © istockphoto / jfelton

Gayle Kowalchyk • E. L. Lancaster
Christine H. Barden

Foreword

Young piano students enjoy playing familiar music. PRE-READING BOOK OF POP was designed for those students who have had only a few weeks of study and consequently have limited skills in note reading.

POSITIONS: Melodies for the pieces are divided between the hands. All positions are shown on the page with the pre-reading notation. Most melodies remain within a single position, but some use accidentals that require movement out of the position. These sharps or flats apply to the same note for the rest of the measure.

RHYTHM: Students may be unfamiliar with the rhythmic notation of some of the pieces. However, they will usually play the music correctly by memory or, if not, the rhythms can be quickly learned by rote.

ACCOMPANIMENTS: Each piece in the book has a duet accompaniment. The accompaniments give the pieces richer sounds and can aid the student with rhythmic security. These pieces make excellent student-teacher or student-parent duets. Both solo and accompaniment parts contain measure numbers for easy reference.

Table of Contents

4

Mickey Mouse March

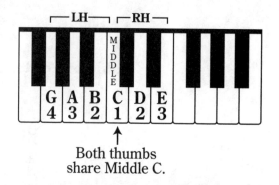

Both thumbs
share Middle C.

Words and Music by Jimmie Dodd
Arr. by Kowalchyk, Lancaster, and Barden

Lively

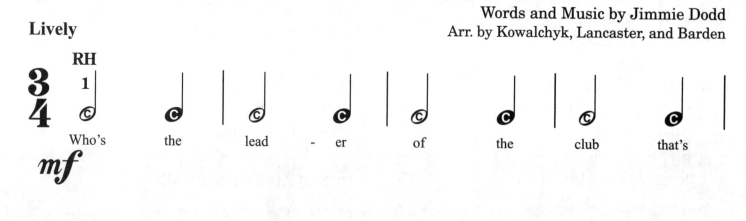

Who's   the   lead - er   of   the   club   that's

5

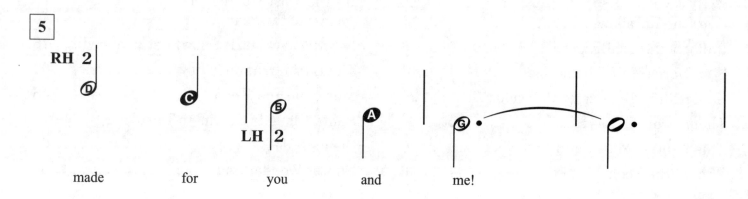

made   for   you   and   me!

Duet Accompaniment: Student plays one octave higher.

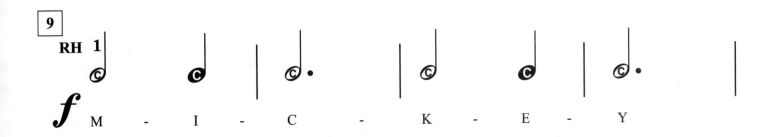

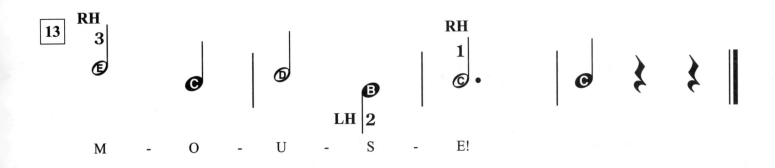

Winnie the Pooh

(from Walt Disney's "The Many Adventures of Winnie the Pooh")

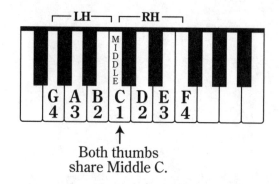

Both thumbs
share Middle C.

Words and Music by
Richard M. Sherman and Robert B. Sherman
Arr. by Kowalchyk, Lancaster, and Barden

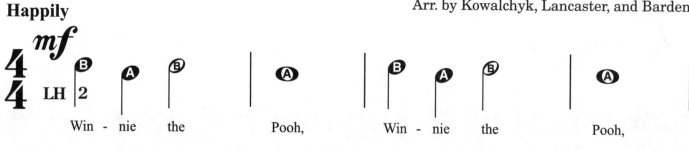

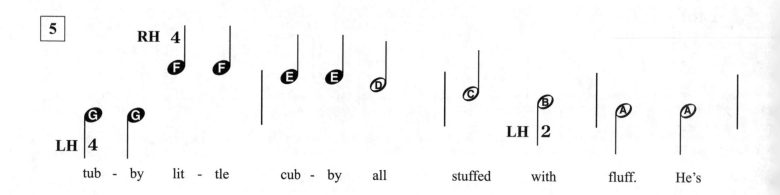

Duet Accompaniment: Student plays one octave higher.

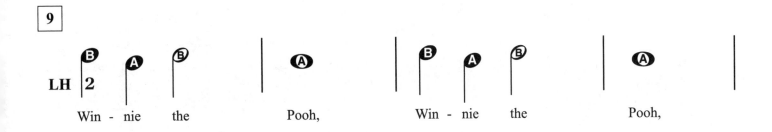

Win - nie the Pooh, Win - nie the Pooh,

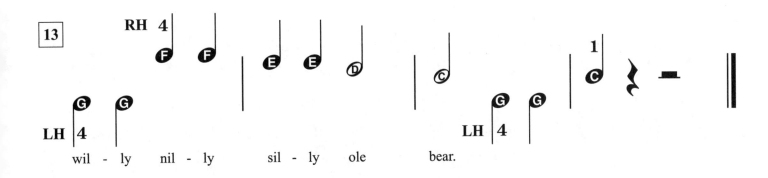

wil - ly nil - ly sil - ly ole bear.

Puff (the Magic Dragon)

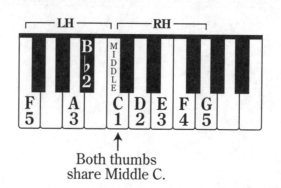

Both thumbs
share Middle C.

Words and Music by
Peter Yarrow and Leonard Lipton
Arr. by Kowalchyk, Lancaster, and Barden

Happily

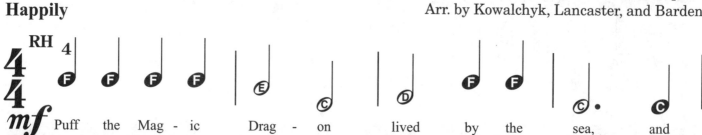

Puff the Mag - ic Drag - on lived by the sea, and

frol - icked in the au - tumn mist in a land called Hon - ah - lee.

Duet Accompaniment: Student plays one octave higher.

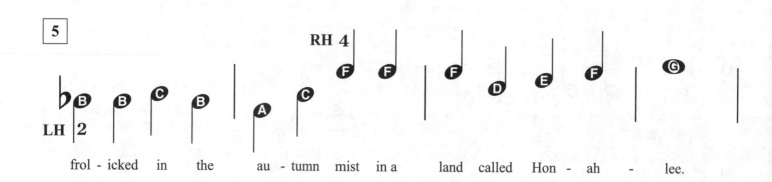

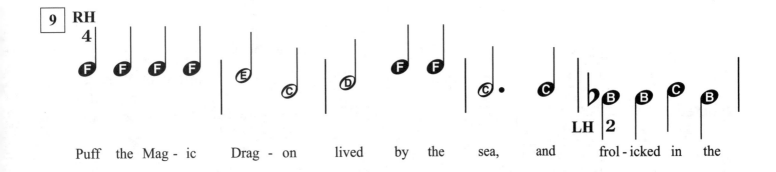

Puff the Mag - ic Drag - on lived by the sea, and frol - icked in the

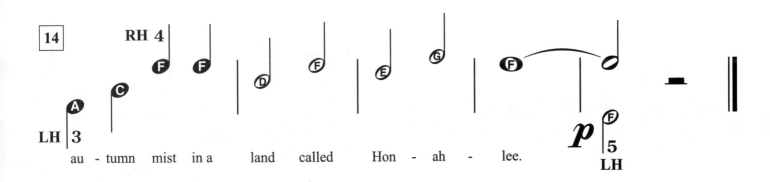

au - tumn mist in a land called Hon - ah - lee.

If I Only Had a Brain

(from the M-G-M Motion Picture
The Wizard of Oz)

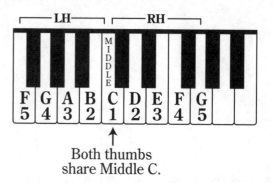

Both thumbs
share Middle C.

Music by Harold Arlen
Lyric by E. Y. Harburg
Arr. by Kowalchyk, Lancaster, and Barden

Relaxed

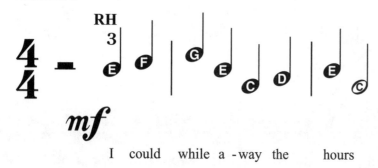

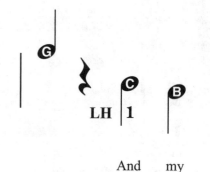

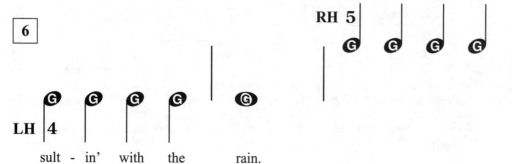

Duet Accompaniment: Student plays one octave higher.

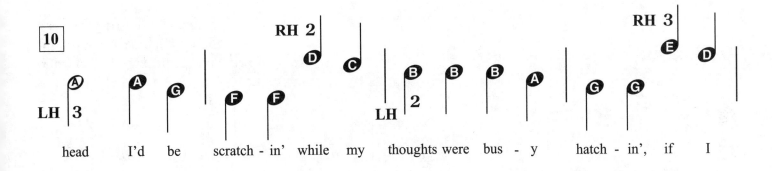

head   I'd   be   scratch - in'   while   my   thoughts were   bus - y   hatch - in',   if   I

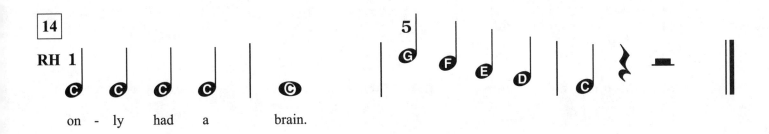

on - ly   had   a   brain.

Hooray for Hollywood

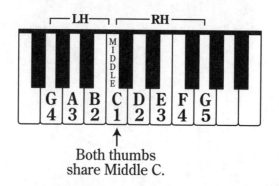

Both thumbs
share Middle C.

Words by Johnny Mercer
Music by Richard A. Whiting
Arr. by Kowalchyk, Lancaster, and Barden

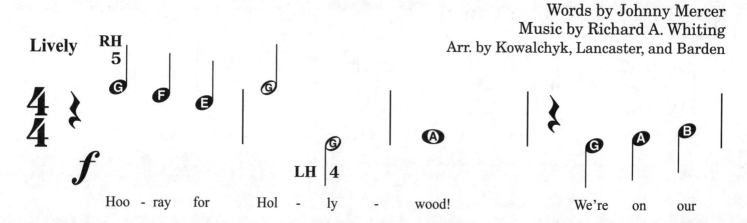

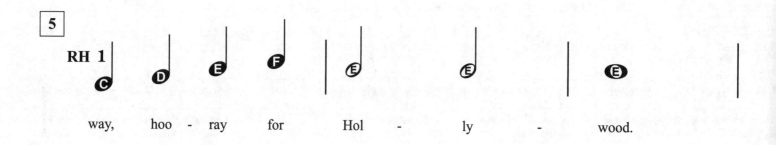

Duet Accompaniment: Student plays one octave higher.

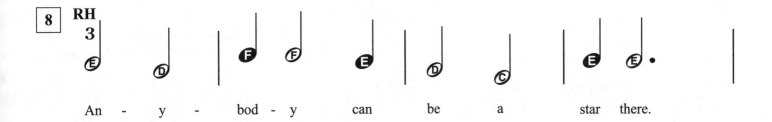

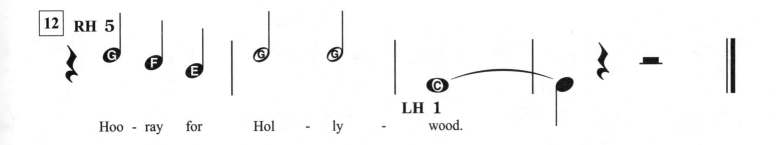

Star Wars
(Main Theme)

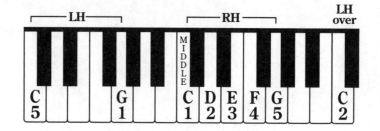

Music by JOHN WILLIAMS
Arr. by Kowalchyk, Lancaster, and Barden

Majestic march tempo

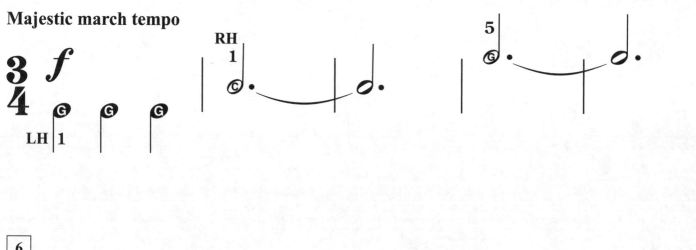

Duet Accompaniment: Student plays one octave higher.

Majestic march tempo

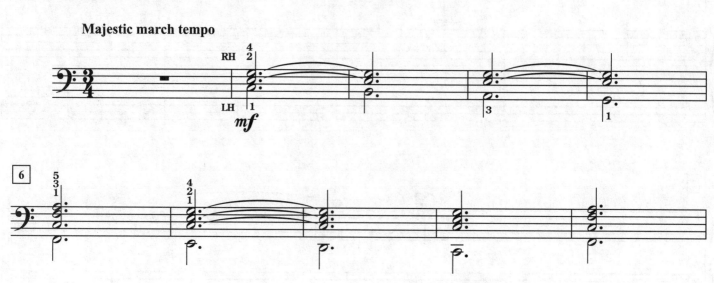

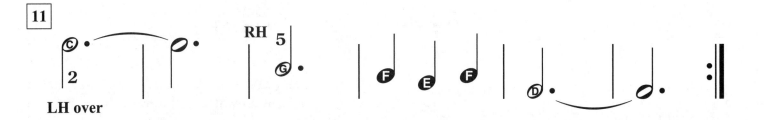

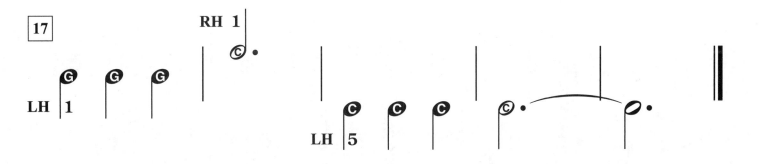

(Meet) The Flintstones

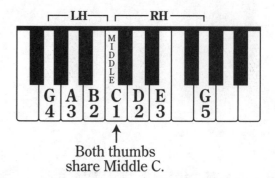

Both thumbs
share Middle C.

Words and Music by
Joseph Barbera, William Hanna, and Hoyt Curtin
Arr. by Kowalchyk, Lancaster, and Barden

Bouncing happily

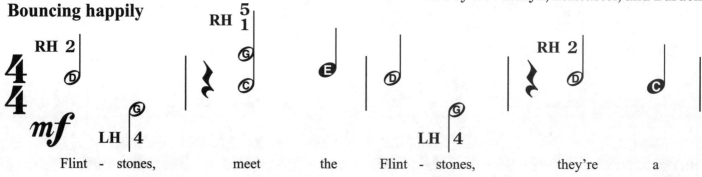

Flint - stones,   meet   the   Flint - stones,   they're   a

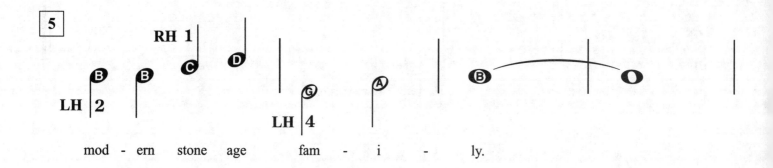

mod - ern   stone   age   fam - i - ly.

Duet Accompaniment: Student plays one octave higher.

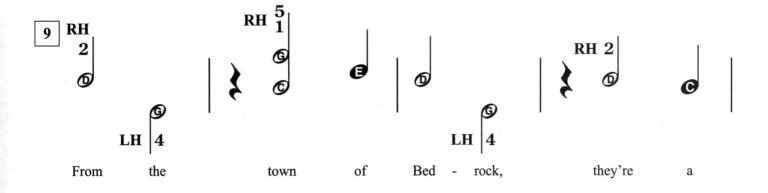

From the town of Bed - rock, they're a

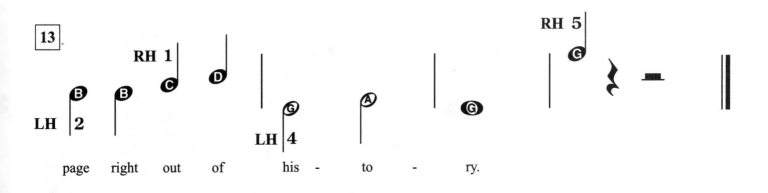

page right out of his - to - ry.

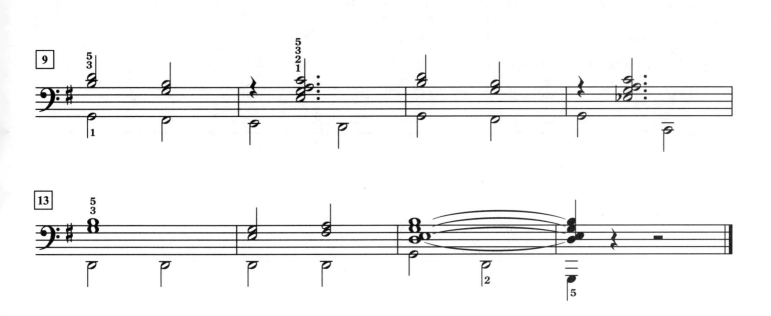

Over the Rainbow

(from the M-G-M Motion Picture
The Wizard of Oz)

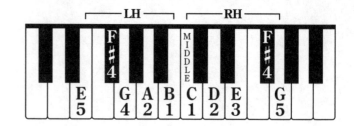

Music by Harold Arlen
Lyric by E. Y. Harburg
Arr. by Kowalchyk, Lancaster, and Barden

Flowing

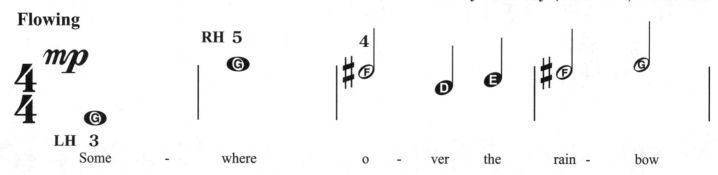

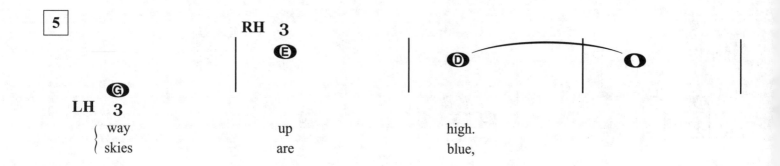

Duet Accompaniment: Student plays one octave higher.

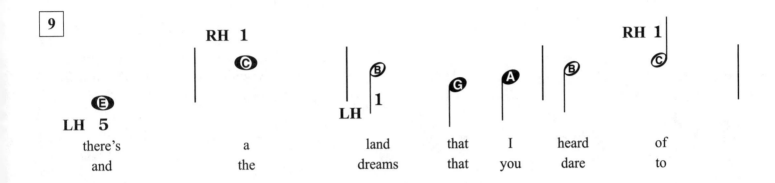

there's / a / land / that / I / heard / of
and / the / dreams / that / you / dare / to

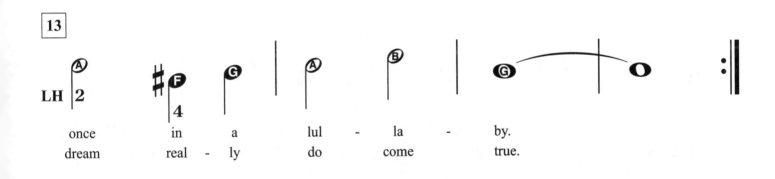

once / in / a / lul - la - by.
dream / real - ly / do / come / true.

Supercalifragilistic-expialidocious

(from Walt Disney's *"Mary Poppins"*)

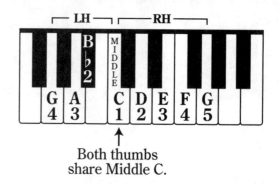

Both thumbs
share Middle C.

Words and Music by
Richard M. Sherman and Robert B. Sherman
Arr. by Kowalchyk, Lancaster, and Barden

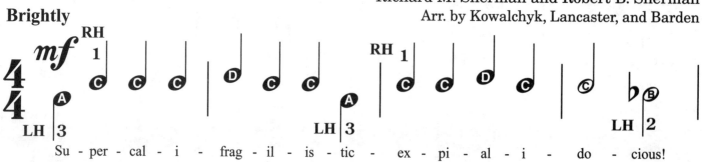

Su - per - cal - i - frag - il - is - tic - ex - pi - al - i - do - cious!

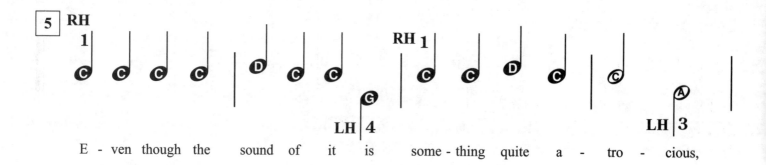

E - ven though the sound of it is some - thing quite a - tro - cious,

Duet Accompaniment: Student plays one octave higher.

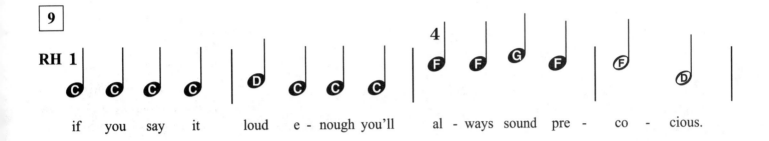

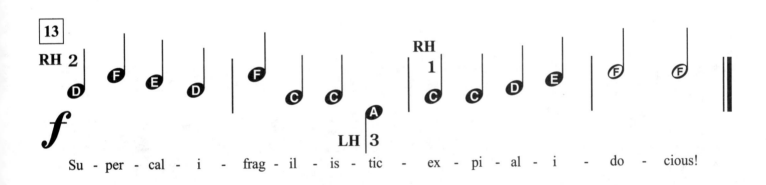

Itsy Bitsy Teenie Weenie Yellow Polka Dot Bikini

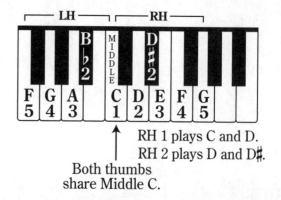

RH 1 plays C and D.
RH 2 plays D and D♯.
Both thumbs
share Middle C.

Words and Music by
Paul J. Vance and Lee Pockriss
Arr. by Kowalchyk, Lancaster, and Barden

Moderately

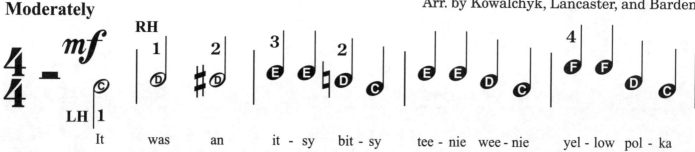

It was an it - sy bit - sy tee - nie wee - nie yel - low pol - ka

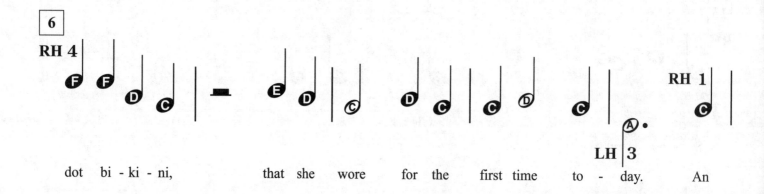

dot bi - ki - ni,   that she wore for the first time to - day. An

Duet Accompaniment: Student plays one octave higher.

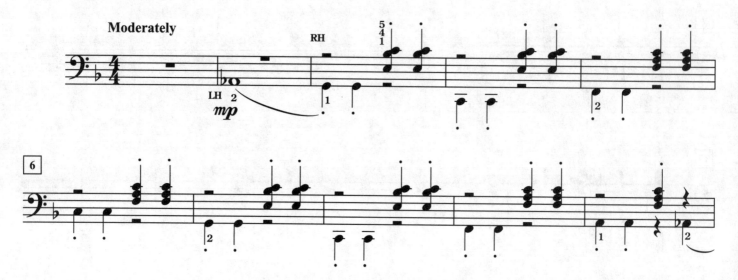

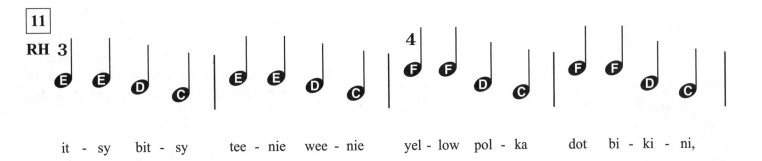

it - sy bit - sy tee - nie wee - nie yel - low pol - ka dot bi - ki - ni,

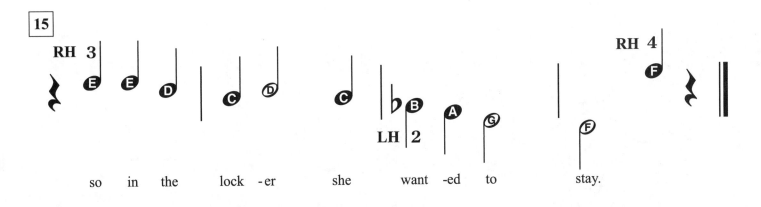

so in the lock - er she want -ed to stay.

It's a Small World

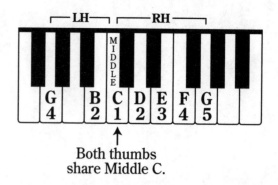

Both thumbs
share Middle C.

Words and Music by
Richard M. Sherman and Robert B. Sherman
Arr. by Kowalchyk, Lancaster, and Barden

Cheerfully

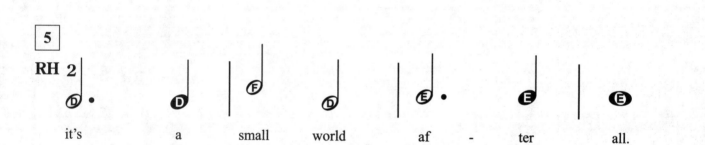

It's   a   small   world   af - ter   all,

mf

it's   a   small   world   af - ter   all.

Duet Accompaniment: Student plays one octave higher.

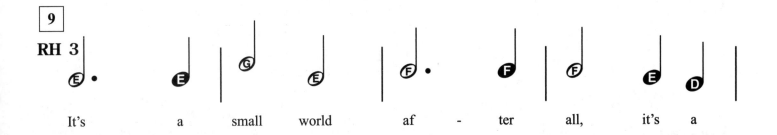

It's   a   small   world   af - ter   all,   it's a

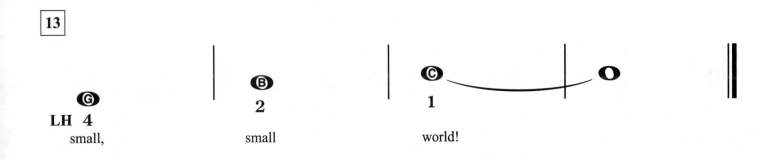

small,   small   world!

This Land Is Your Land

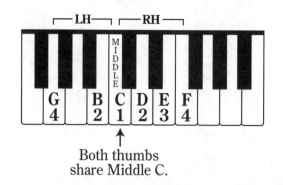

Both thumbs
share Middle C.

Words and Music by Woody Guthrie
Arr. by Kowalchyk, Lancaster, and Barden

Moderately fast

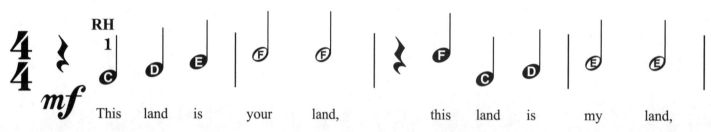

This   land   is   your   land,   this   land   is   my   land,

5

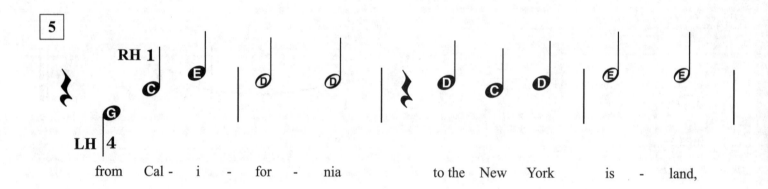

from   Cal - i - for - nia   to the   New   York   is - land,

Duet Accompaniment: Student plays one octave higher.

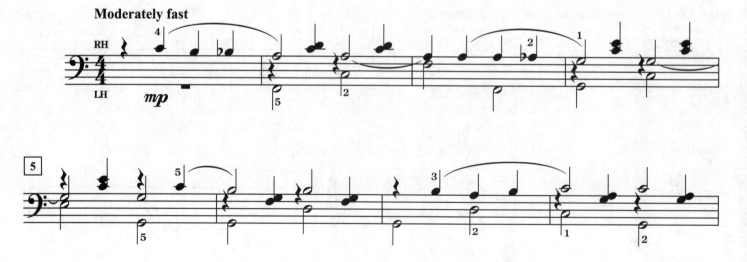

from the red - wood   for - est   to the Gulf Stream   wa   -   ters,

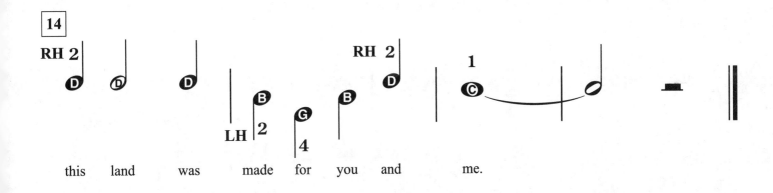

this   land   was   made   for   you   and   me.

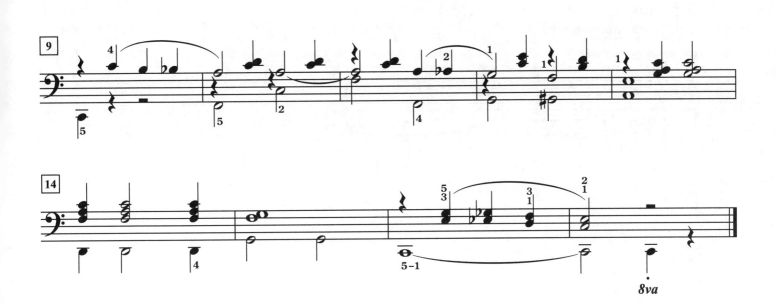

8va

The Lion Sleeps Tonight

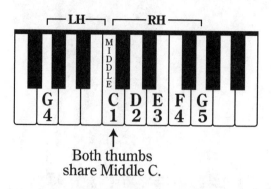

Both thumbs
share Middle C.

New Lyric and Revised Music by
George David Weiss, Hugo Peretti, and Luigi Creatore
Arr. by Kowalchyk, Lancaster, and Barden

Moderate, with courage

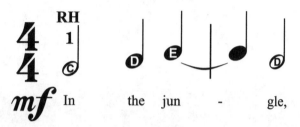
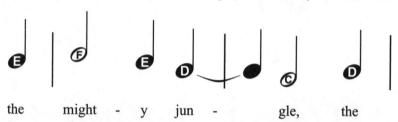

In the jun - gle, the might - y jun - gle, the
li - on sleeps to - night.

Duet Accompaniment: Student plays one octave higher.

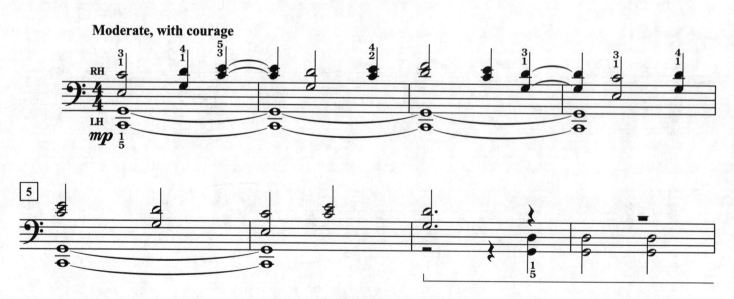

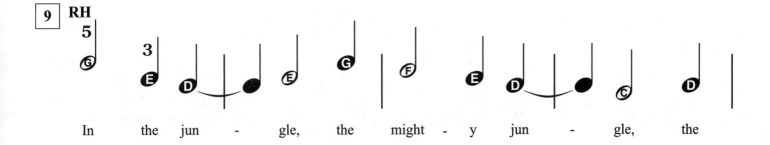

In the jun - gle, the might - y jun - gle, the

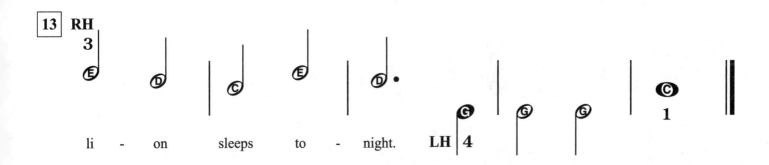

li - on sleeps to - night. **LH** 4

The Chicken Dance
(Dance Little Bird)

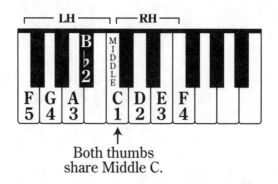

Both thumbs
share Middle C.

Music by Terry Rendall and Werner Thomas
English Lyrics by Paul Parnes
Arr. by Kowalchyk, Lancaster, and Barden

Fast and clucky

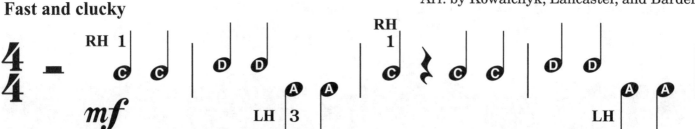

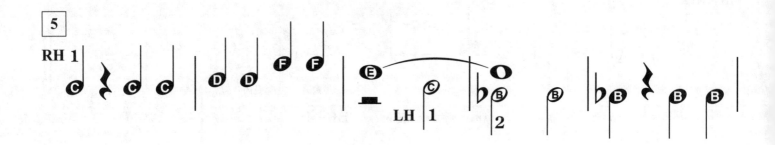

Duet Accompaniment: Student plays one octave higher.

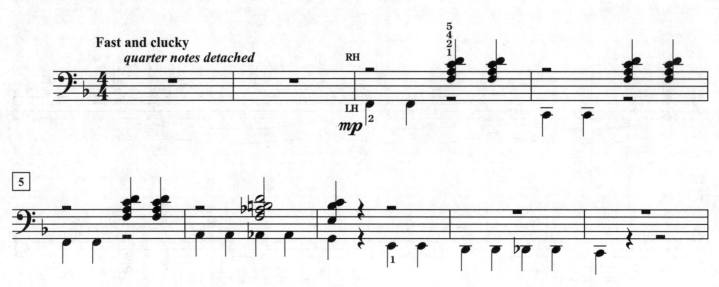

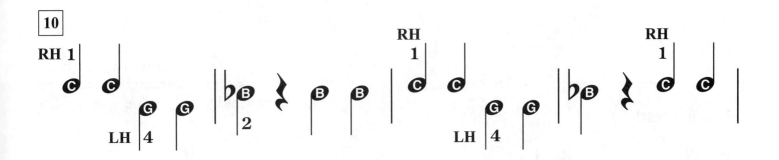

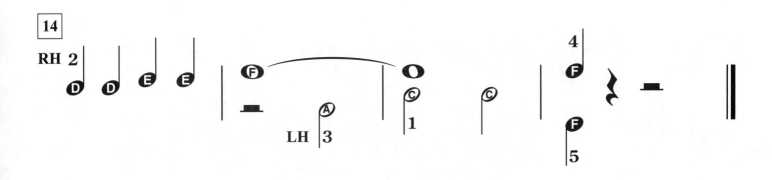

Inspector Gadget
(Main Title)

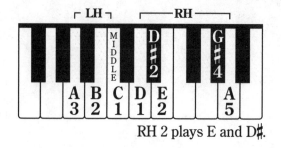

RH 2 plays E and D♯.

Words and Music by
Haim Saban and Shuki Levy
Arr. by Kowalchyk, Lancaster, and Barden

Moving fast!

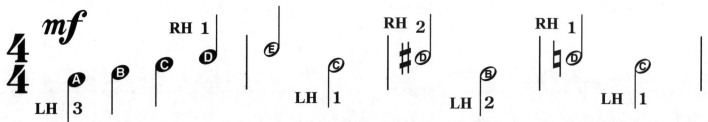

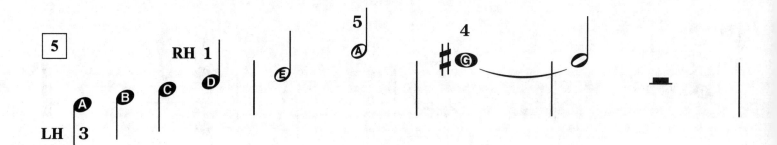

Duet Accompaniment: Student plays one octave higher.

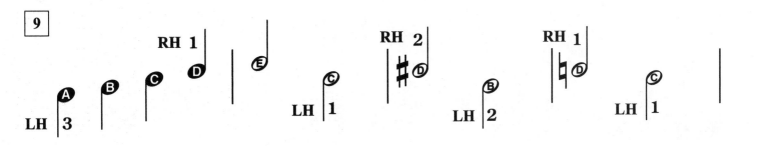

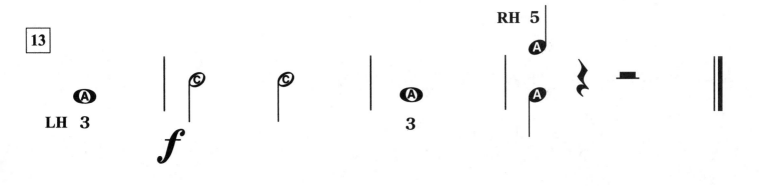

Theme from "Superman"

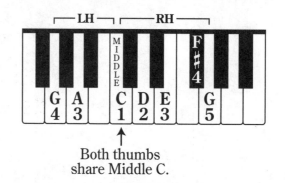

By JOHN WILLIAMS
Arr. by Kowalchyk, Lancaster, and Barden

Moderately fast

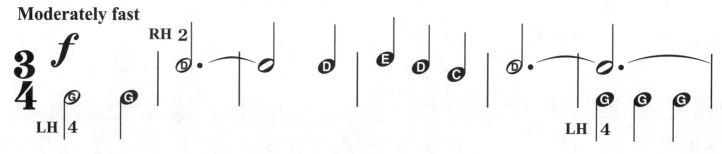

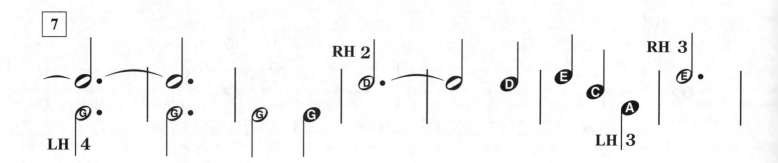

Duet Accompaniment: Student plays one octave higher.

Moderately fast

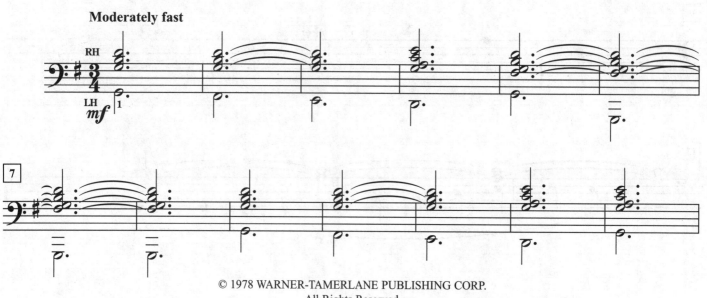

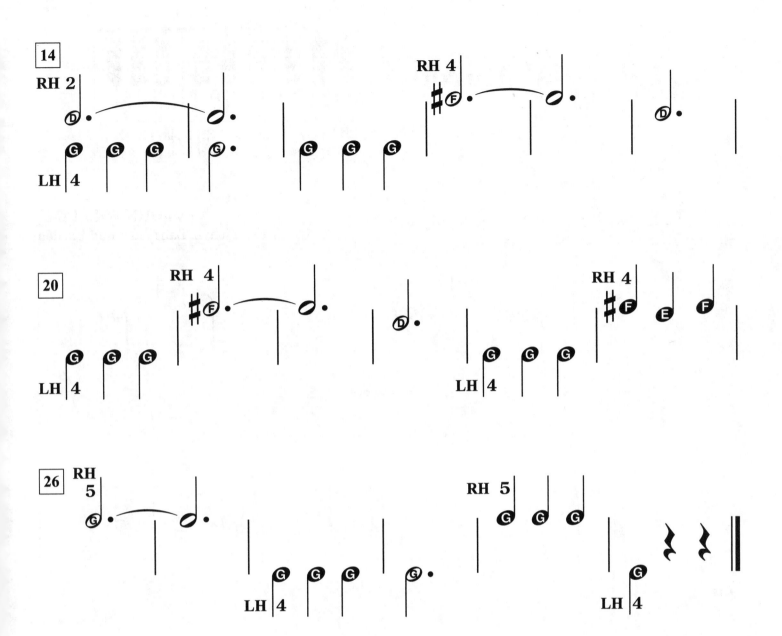

The Imperial March

(Darth Vader's Theme)

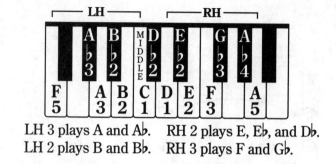

LH 3 plays A and A♭.   RH 2 plays E, E♭, and D♭.
LH 2 plays B and B♭.   RH 3 plays F and G♭.

By JOHN WILLIAMS
Arr. by Kowalchyk, Lancaster, and Barden

Boldly

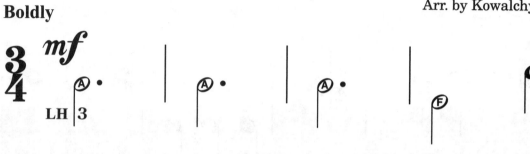

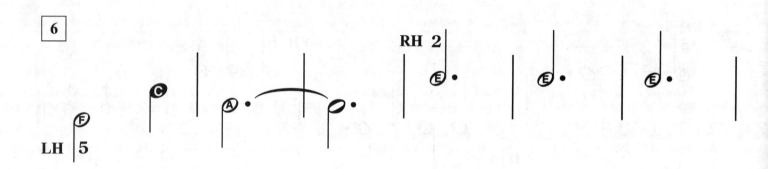

Duet Accompaniment: Student plays one octave higher.

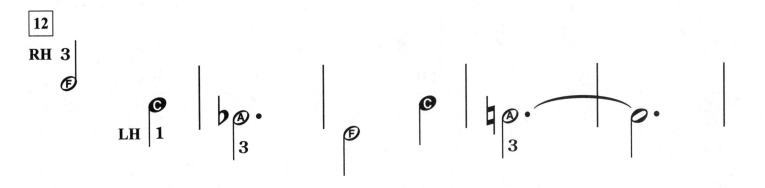

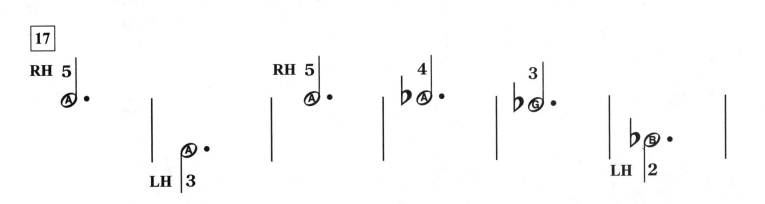

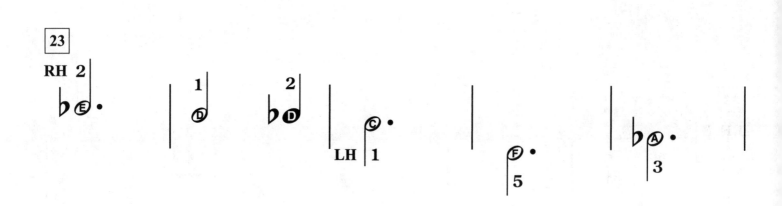

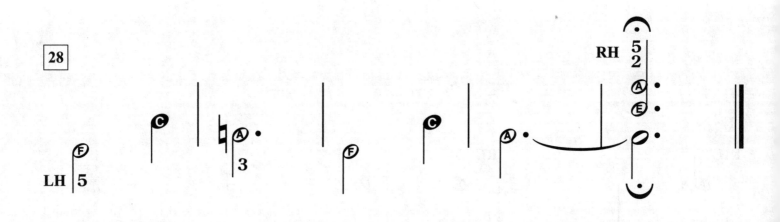

Here I Am to Worship
(Light of the World)

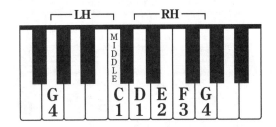

Words and Music by Tim Hughes
Arr. by Kowalchyk and Lancaster

Moderately

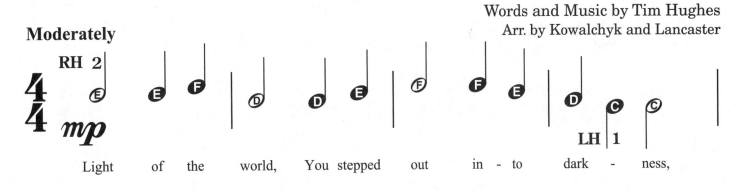

Light of the world, You stepped out in - to dark - ness,

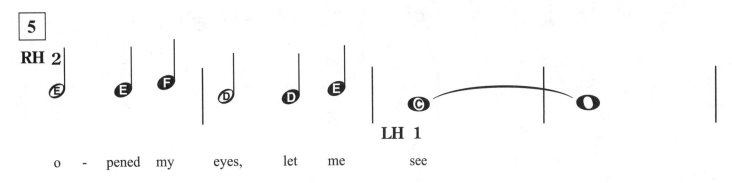

o - pened my eyes, let me see

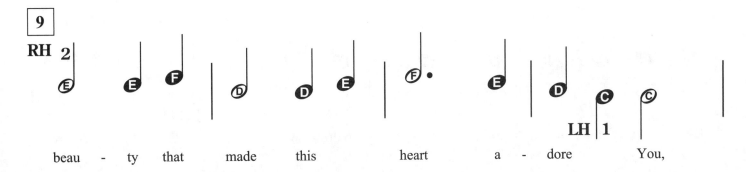

beau - ty that made this heart a - dore You,

Duet Accompaniment: Student plays one octave higher.

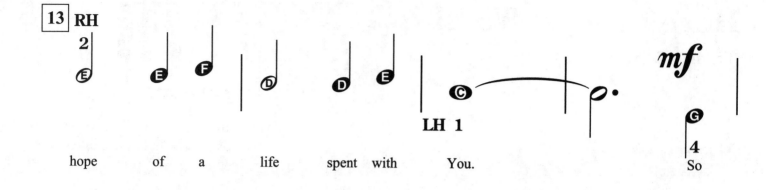

hope   of   a   life   spent with   You.   So

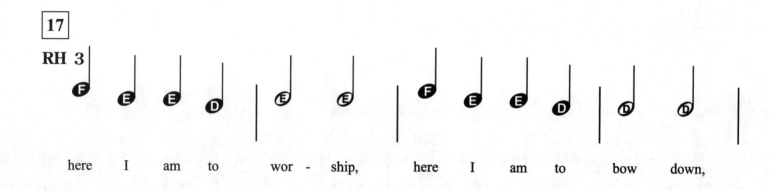

here   I   am   to   wor - ship,   here   I   am   to   bow   down,

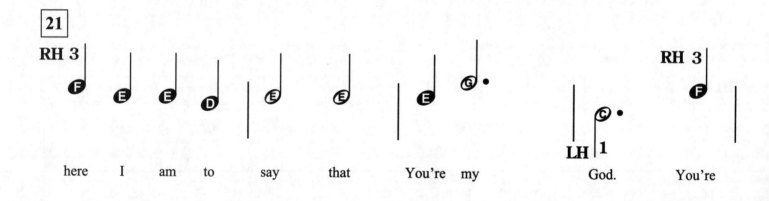

here   I   am   to   say   that   You're   my   God.   You're

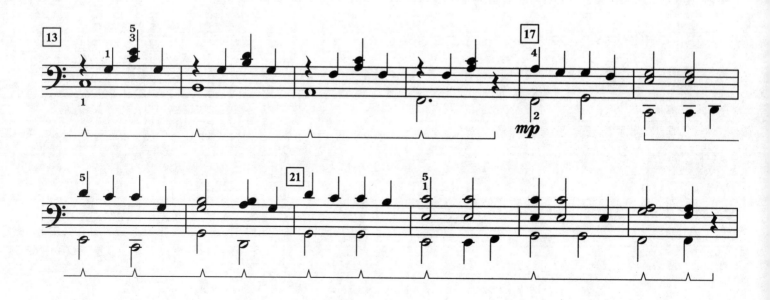

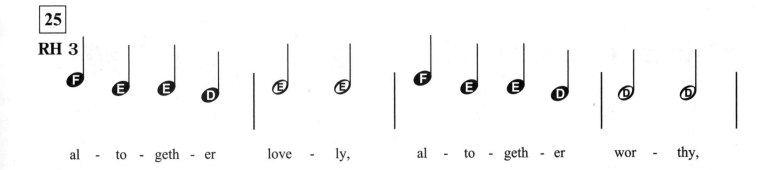

al - to - geth - er love - ly, al - to - geth - er wor - thy,

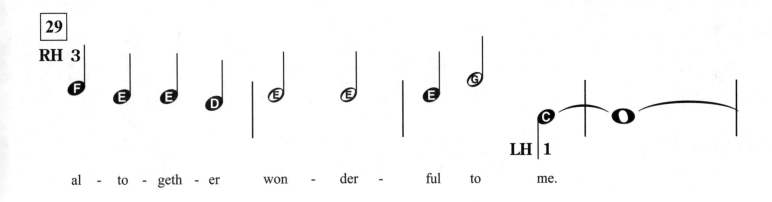

al - to - geth - er won - der - ful to me.

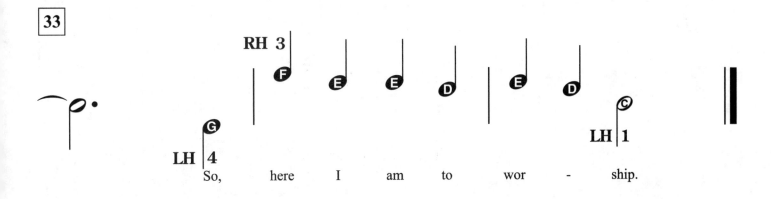

So, here I am to wor - ship.

Shout to the North

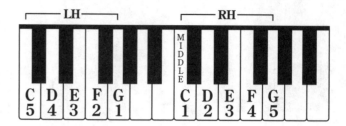

Words and Music by Martin Smith
Arr. by Kowalchyk and Lancaster

Flowing waltz tempo

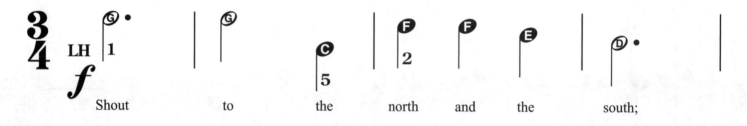

Shout   to   the   north   and   the   south;

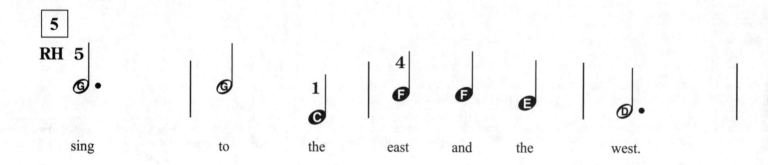

sing   to   the   east   and   the   west.

Duet Accompaniment: Student plays one octave higher.

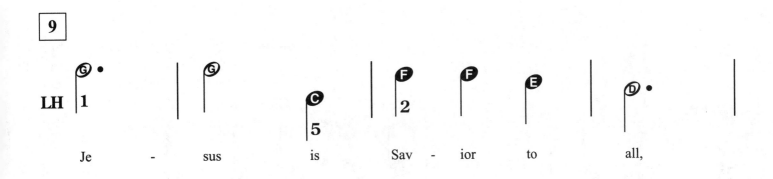

Je - sus is Sav - ior to all,

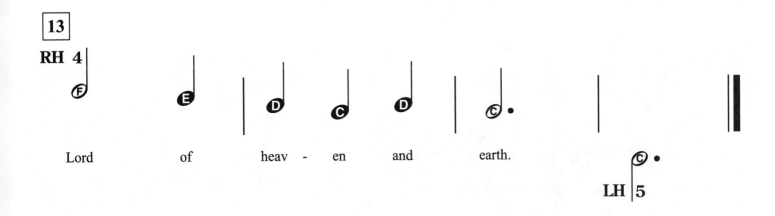

Lord of heav - en and earth.

Because He Lives

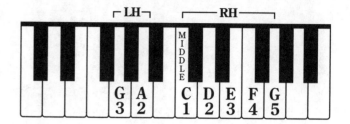

Words by William J. and Gloria Gaither
Music by William J. Gaither
Arr. by Kowalchyk and Lancaster

Joyfully

Duet Accompaniment: Student plays one octave higher.

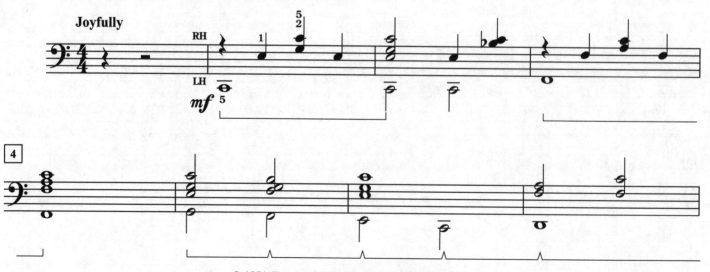

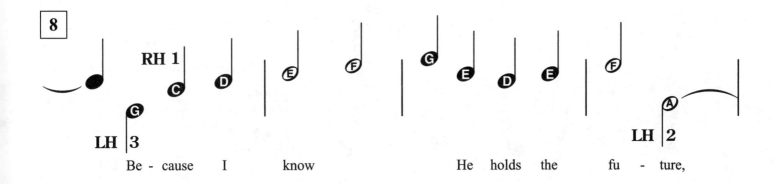

Be - cause I know He holds the fu - ture,

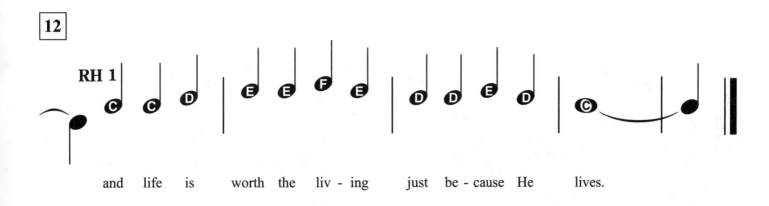

and life is worth the liv - ing just be - cause He lives.

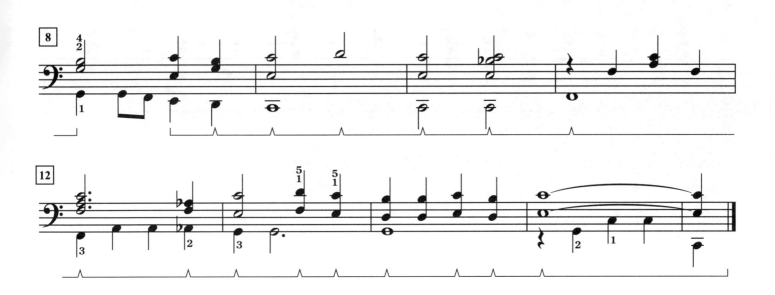

Worthy Is the Lamb

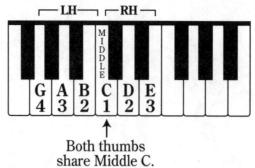

Words and Music by
Darlene Zschech
Arr. by Kowalchyk and Lancaster

Moderately

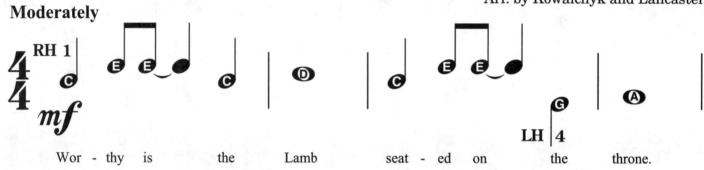

Wor - thy is the Lamb seat - ed on the throne.

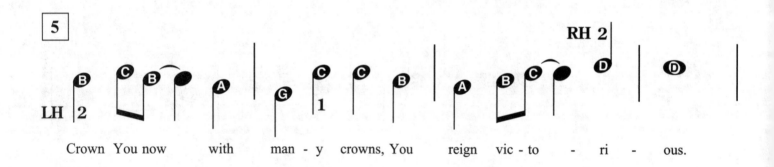

Crown You now with man - y crowns, You reign vic - to - ri - ous.

Duet Accompaniment: Student plays one octave higher.

Moderately

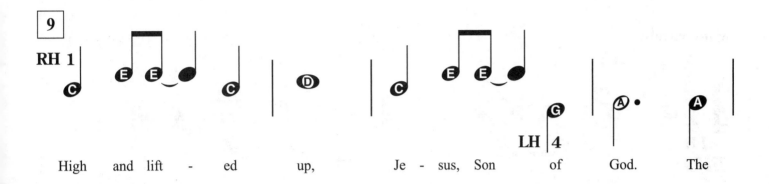

High and lift - ed up, Je - sus, Son of God. The

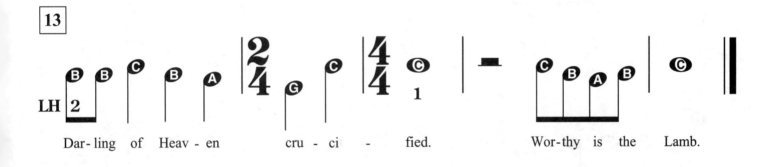

Dar - ling of Heav - en cru - ci - fied. Wor-thy is the Lamb.

How Great Is Our God

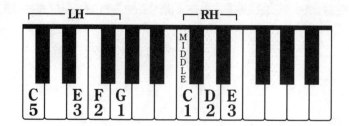

Words and Music by
Jesse Reeves, Chris Tomlin and Ed Cash
Arr. by Kowalchyk and Lancaster

Moderately

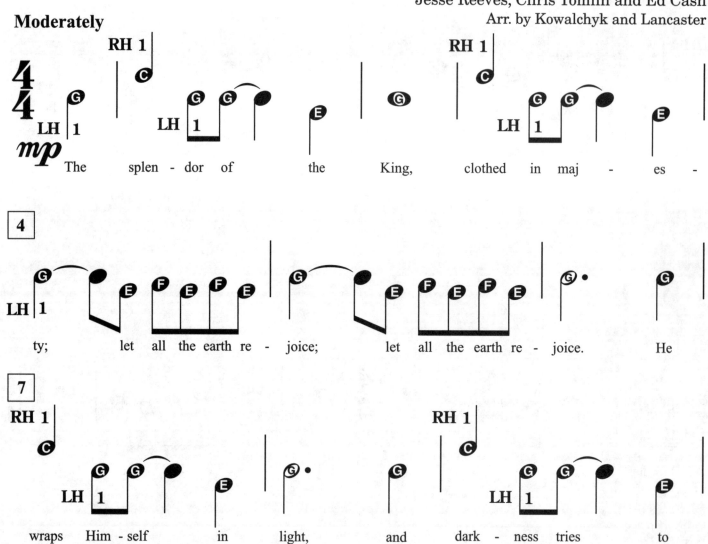

The splen-dor of the King, clothed in maj-es-ty; let all the earth re-joice; let all the earth re-joice. He wraps Him-self in light, and dark-ness tries to

Duet Accompaniment: Student plays one octave higher.

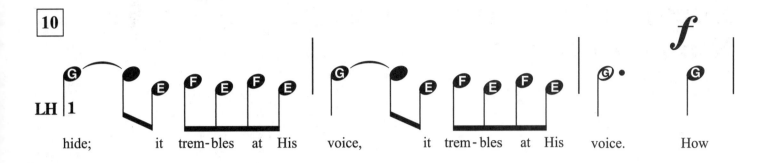

hide; it trem-bles at His voice, it trem-bles at His voice. How

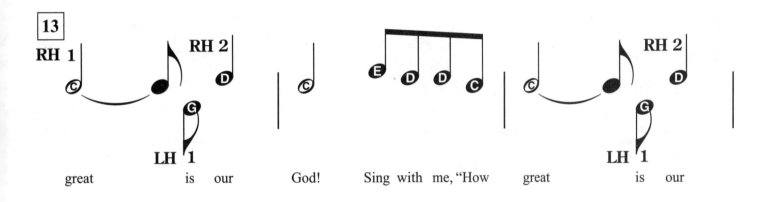

great is our God! Sing with me, "How great is our

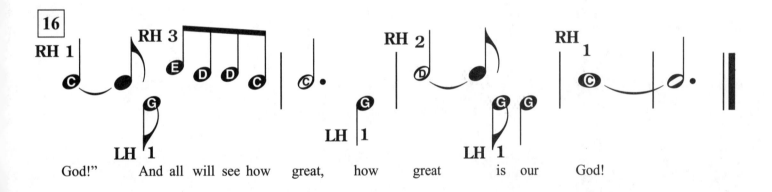

God!" And all will see how great, how great is our God!

Lord, I Lift Your Name on High

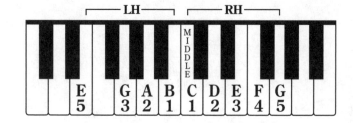

Words and Music by Rick Founds
Arr. by Kowalchyk and Lancaster

Moderately

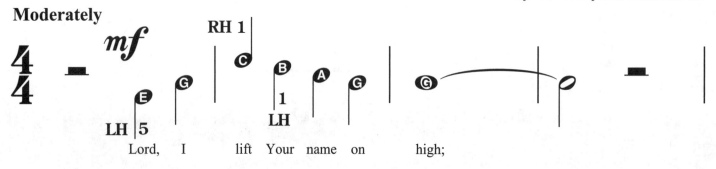

Lord, I lift Your name on high;

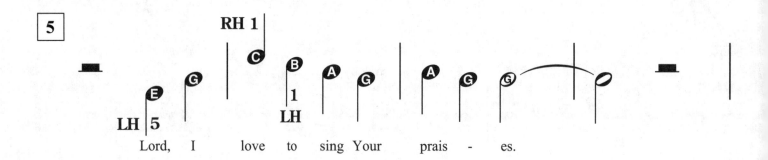

Lord, I love to sing Your prais - es.

Duet Accompaniment: Student plays one octave higher.

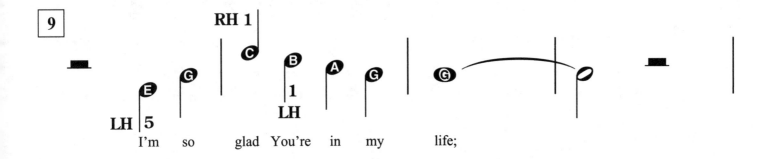

I'm so glad You're in my life;

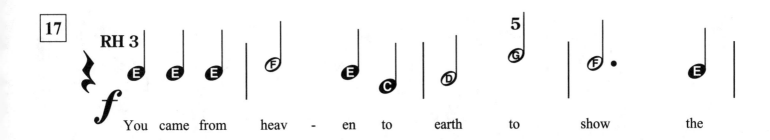

I'm so glad You came to save us.

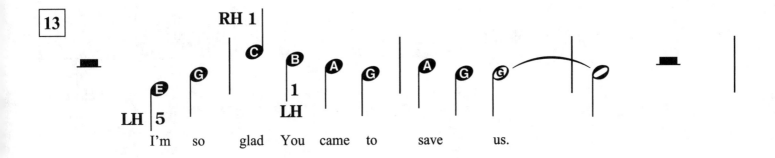

You came from heav - en to earth to show the

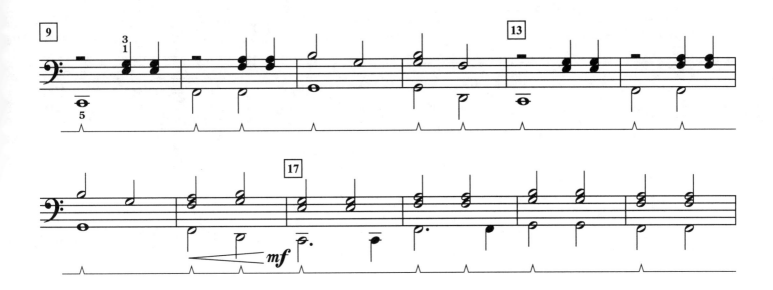

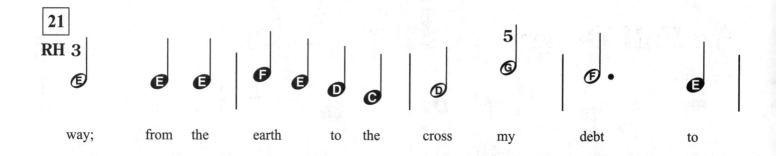

way;   from   the   earth   to   the   cross   my   debt   to

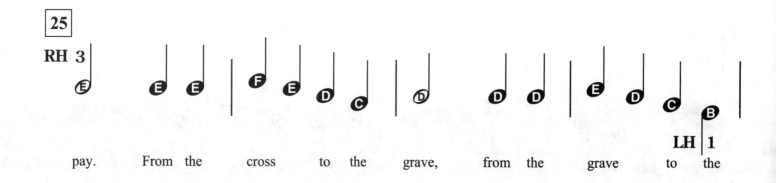

pay.   From   the   cross   to   the   grave,   from   the   grave   to   the

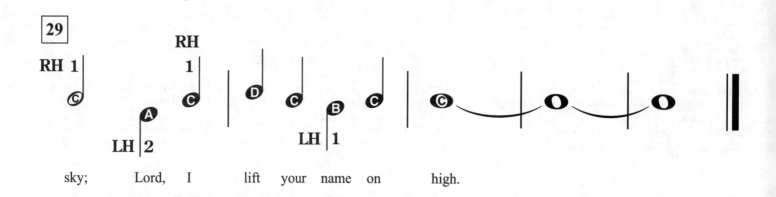

sky;   Lord,   I   lift   your   name   on   high.

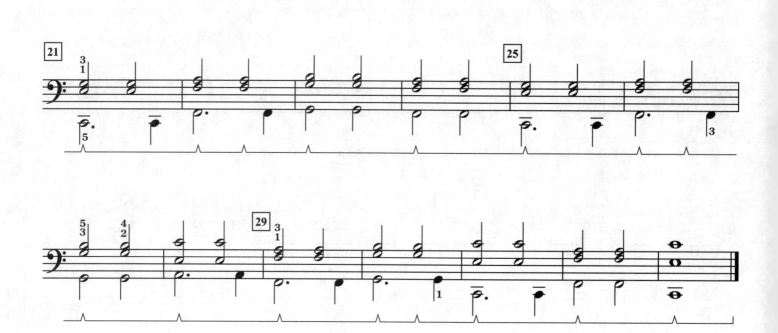

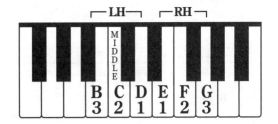

We Fall Down

Words and Music by Chris Tomlin
Arr. by Kowalchyk and Lancaster

Moderately fast (in 2)

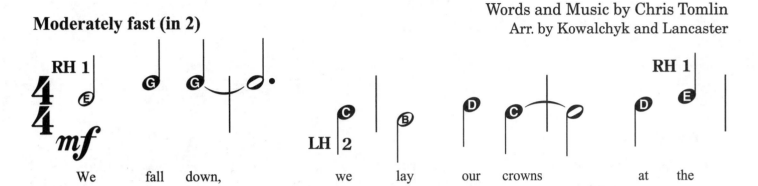

We fall down, we lay our crowns at the

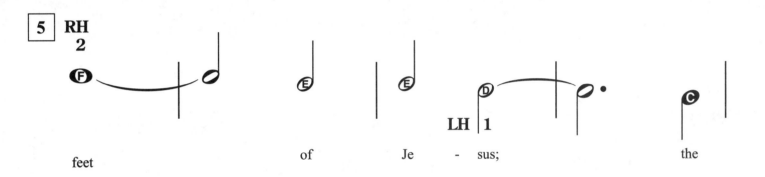

feet of Je - sus; the

Duet Accompaniment: Student plays one octave higher.

Moderately fast (in 2)

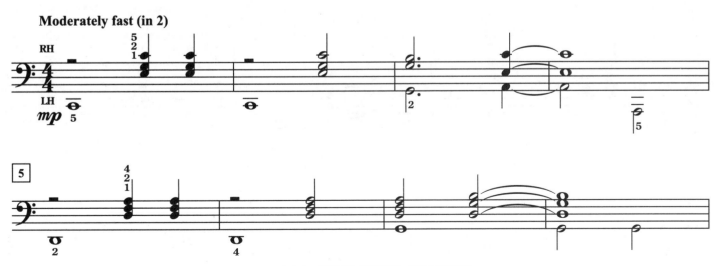

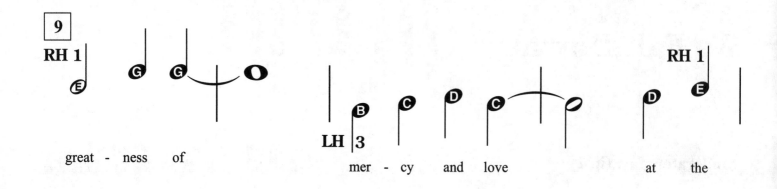

great - ness of mer - cy and love at the

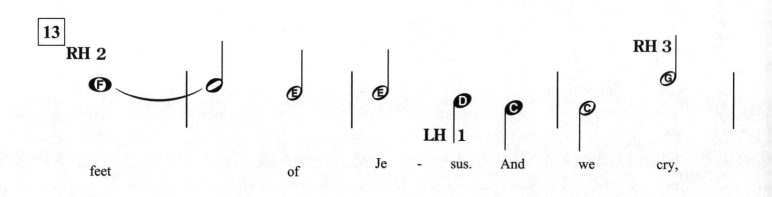

feet of Je - sus. And we cry,

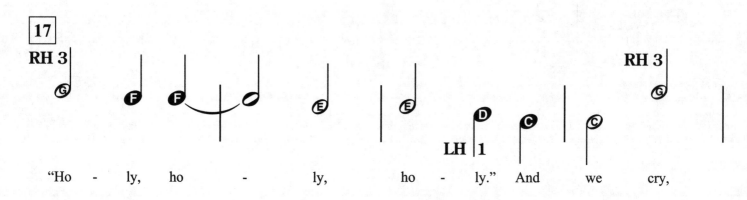

"Ho - ly, ho - ly, ho - ly." And we cry,

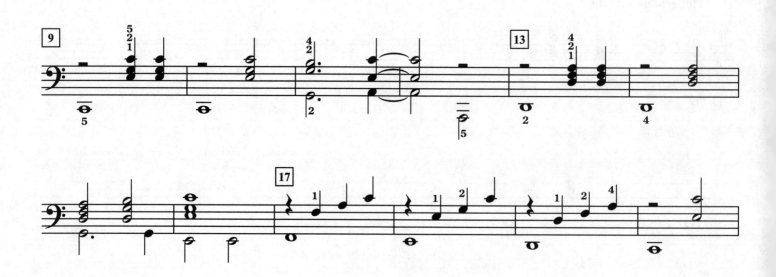

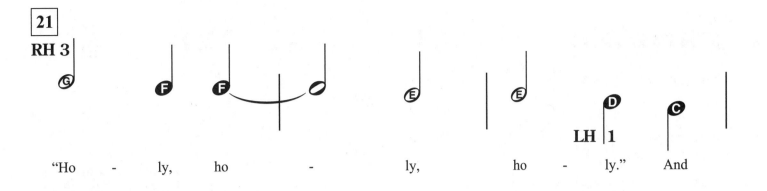

"Ho - ly, ho - ly, ho - ly." And

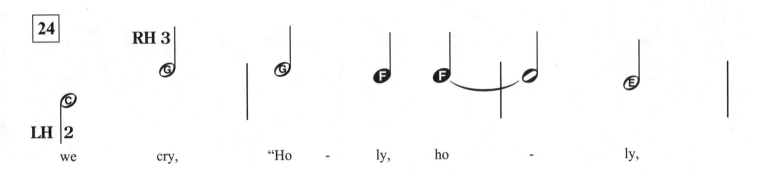

we cry, "Ho - ly, ho - ly,

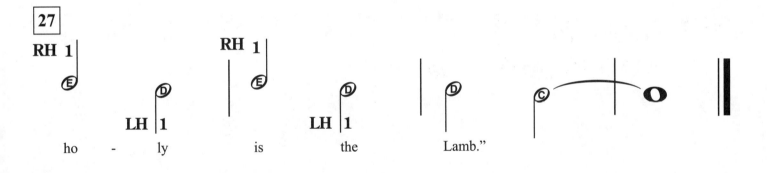

ho - ly is the Lamb."

Mary, Did You Know?

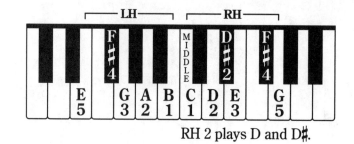

RH 2 plays D and D♯.

Words and Music by
Mark Lowry and Buddy Greene
Arr. by Kowalchyk and Lancaster

Moderately

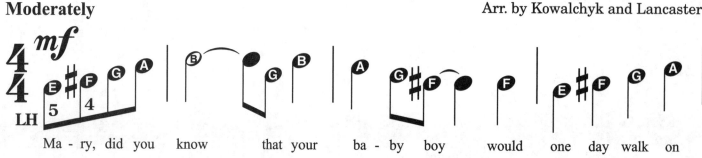

Ma - ry, did you know that your ba - by boy would one day walk on

wa - ter? Ma - ry, did you know that your ba - by boy would

Duet Accompaniment: Student plays one octave higher.

Moderately

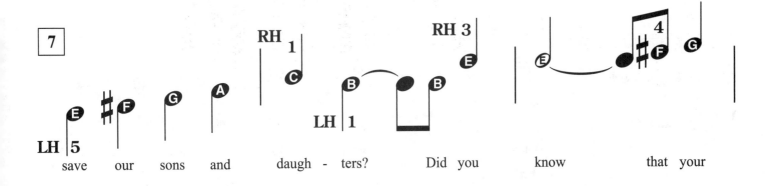

7 save our sons and daugh - ters? Did you know that your

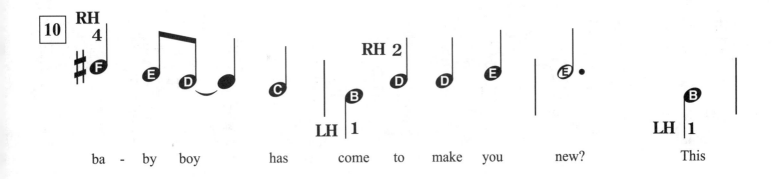

10 ba - by boy has come to make you new? This

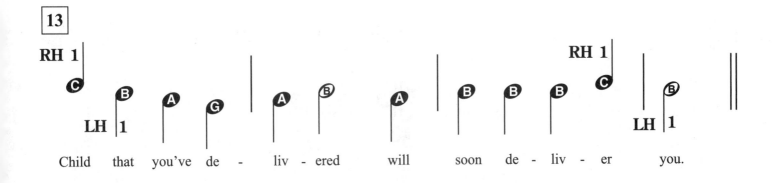

13 Child that you've de - liv - ered will soon de - liv - er you.

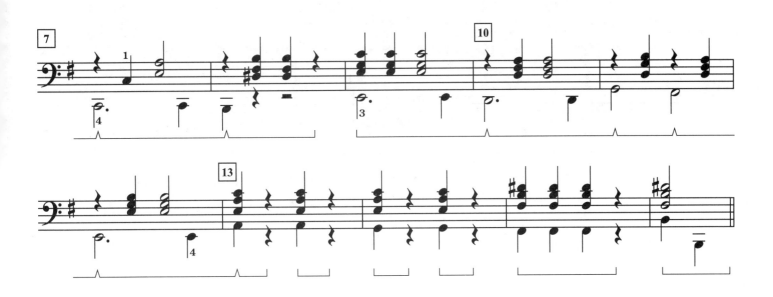

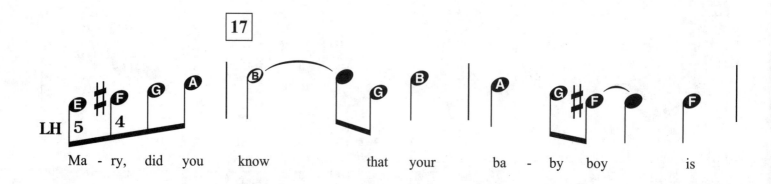

17

Ma - ry, did you know that your ba - by boy is

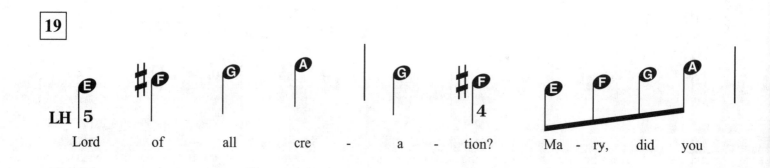

19

Lord of all cre - a - tion? Ma - ry, did you

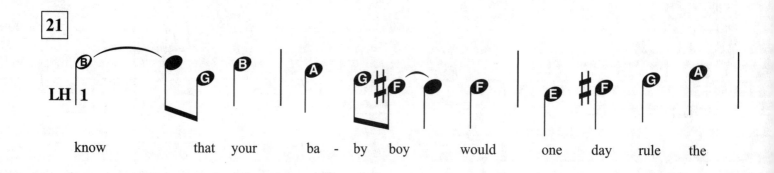

21

know that your ba - by boy would one day rule the

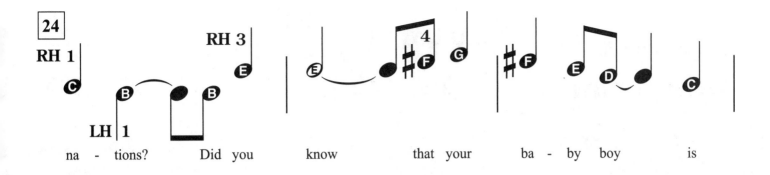

na - tions? Did you know that your ba - by boy is

heav - en's per - fect Lamb? And the sleep - ing Child you're

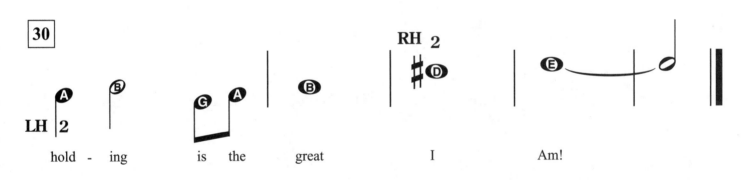

hold - ing is the great I Am!

Winter Wonderland

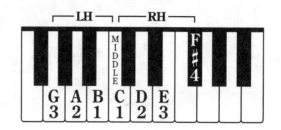

Words by Dick Smith
Music by Felix Bernard
Arr. by Kowalchyk and Lancaster

Moderately fast

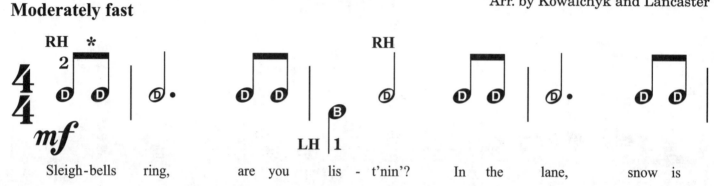

Sleigh-bells ring, are you lis - t'nin'? In the lane, snow is glis - t'nin'. A beau - ti - ful sight, we're hap - py to - night,

* **Optional:** The pairs of eighth notes may be performed in swing style.

Duet Accompaniment: Student plays one octave higher.

Moderately fast

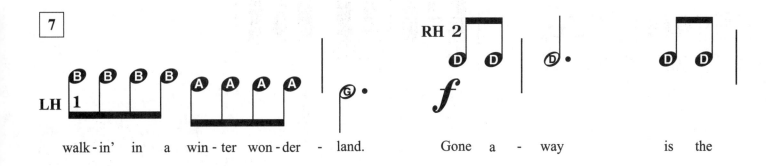

walk-in' in a win-ter won-der - land. Gone a - way is the

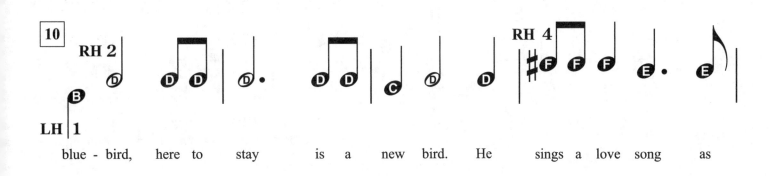

blue - bird, here to stay is a new bird. He sings a love song as

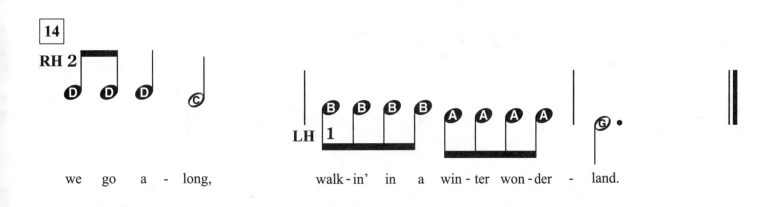

we go a - long, walk-in' in a win-ter won-der - land.

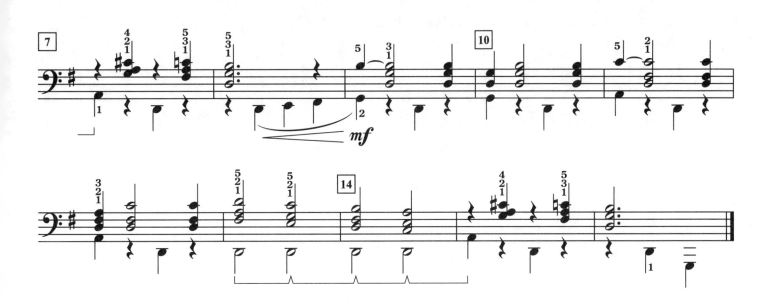

Sleigh Ride

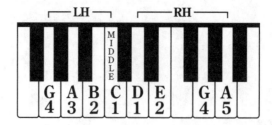

Music by Leroy Anderson
Words by Mitchell Parish
Arr. by Kowalchyk and Lancaster

With energy

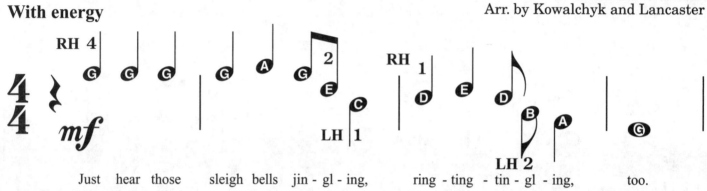

Just hear those sleigh bells jin - gl - ing, ring - ting - tin - gl - ing, too.

Come on, it's love - ly weath - er for a sleigh ride to - geth - er with you.

Duet Accompaniment: Student plays one octave higher.

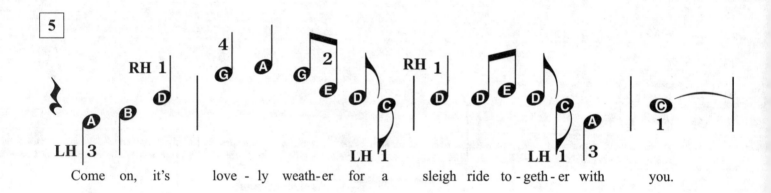

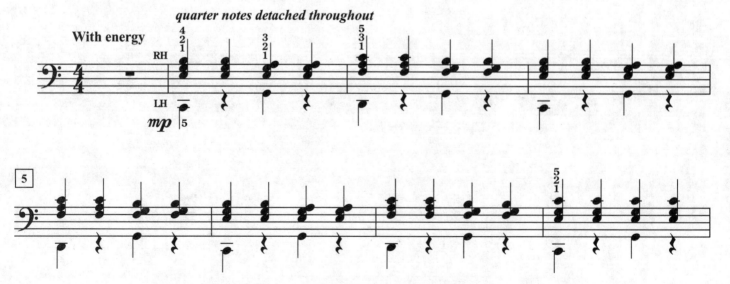

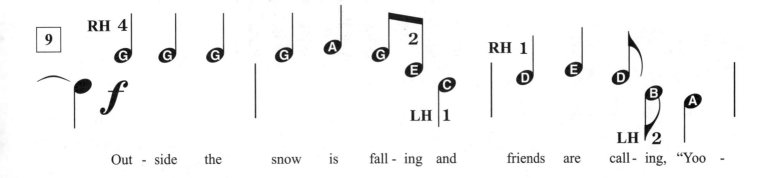

Out - side   the   snow   is   fall - ing   and   friends   are   call - ing, "Yoo -

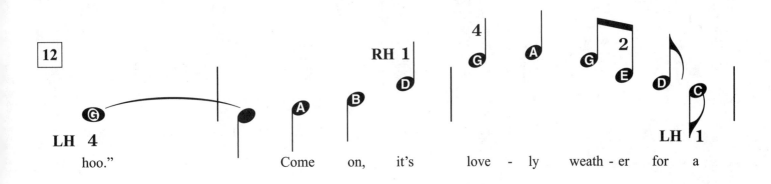

hoo."   Come   on,   it's   love - ly   weath - er   for   a

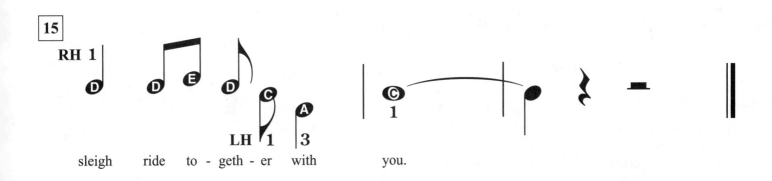

sleigh   ride   to - geth - er   with   you.

Frosty the Snowman

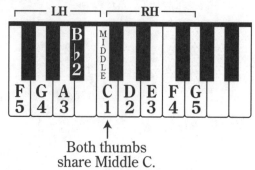

Both thumbs
share Middle C.

Words and Music by
Steve Nelson and Jack Rollins
Arr. by Kowalchyk and Lancaster

Moderately fast

Frost - y the Snow-man was a jol - ly, hap - py soul, with a
Frost - y the Snow-man is a fair - y tale they say, he was

corn - cob pipe and a but - ton nose and two eyes made out of coal.
made of snow, but the chil - dren know how he

Duet Accompaniment: Student plays one octave higher.

Moderately fast

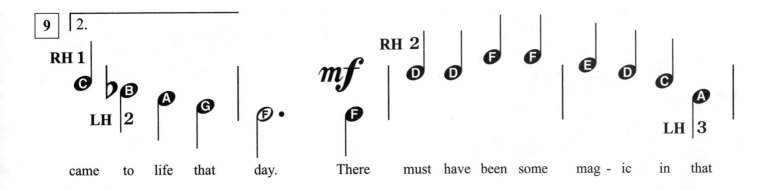

came to life that day. There must have been some mag - ic in that

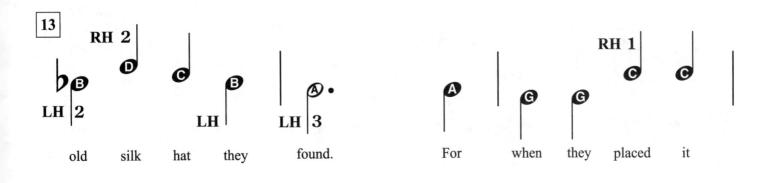

old silk hat they found. For when they placed it

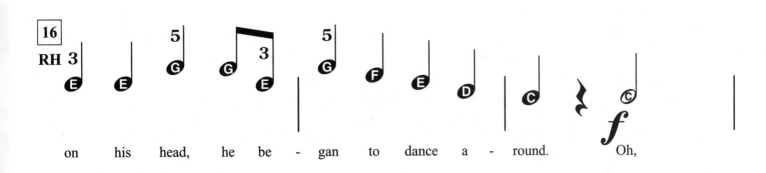

on his head, he be - gan to dance a - round. Oh,

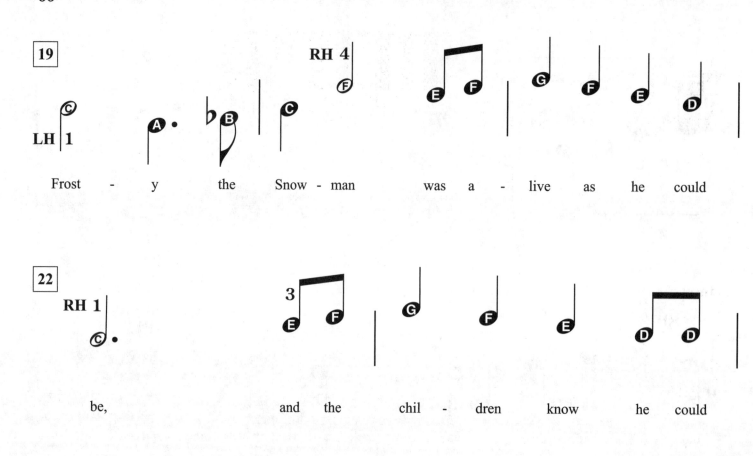

Frost - y the Snow - man was a - live as he could

be, and the chil - dren know he could

laugh and play just the same as you and me.

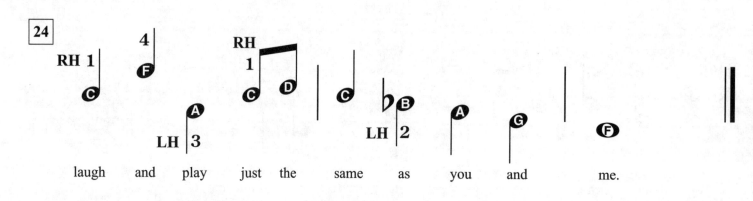

The Little Drummer Boy

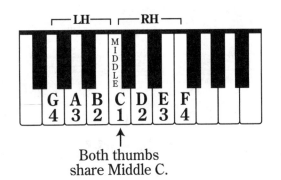

Both thumbs
share Middle C.

Words and Music by
Harry Simeone, Henry Onorati and Katherine Davis
Arr. by Kowalchyk and Lancaster

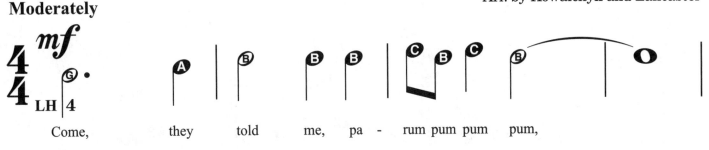

Come, they told me, pa - rum pum pum pum,

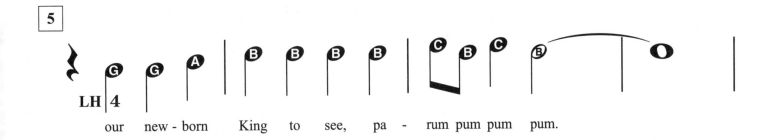

our new - born King to see, pa - rum pum pum pum.

Duet Accompaniment: Student plays one octave higher.

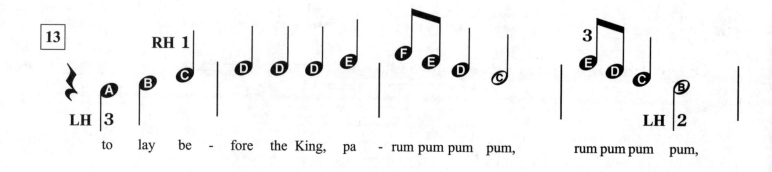

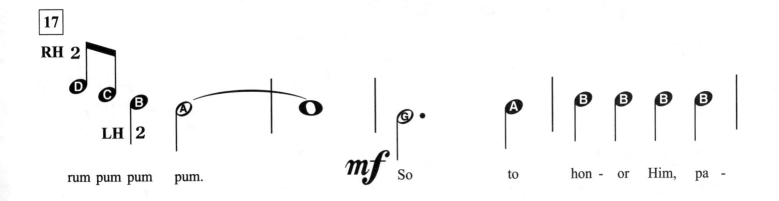

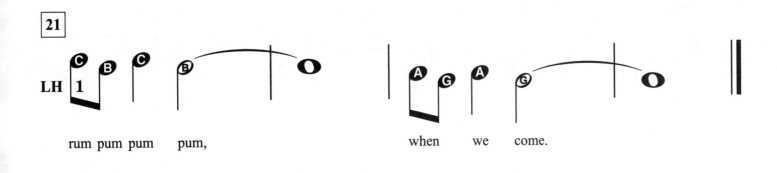

rum pum pum pum. *mf* So to hon - or Him, pa -

rum pum pum pum, when we come.

It's the Most Wonderful Time of the Year

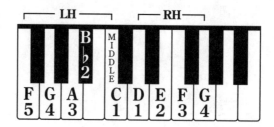

Words and Music by
Eddie Pola and George Wyle
Arr. by Kowalchyk and Lancaster

Bright waltz tempo

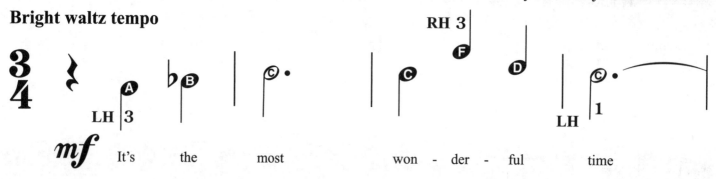

It's the most won - der - ful time

5

of the year. With the

Duet Accompaniment: Student plays one octave higher.

Bright waltz tempo

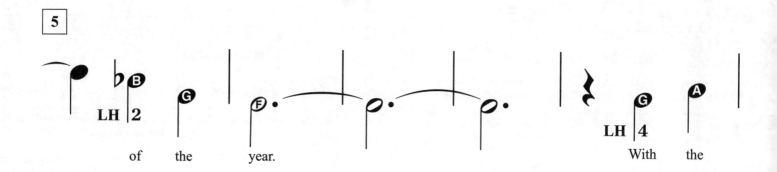

5

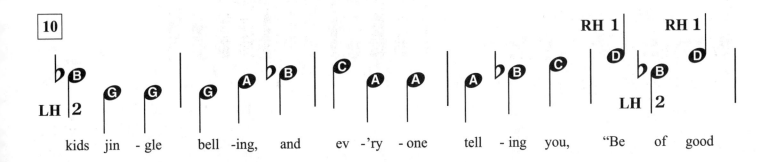

kids jin - gle bell -ing, and ev -'ry -one tell -ing you, "Be of good

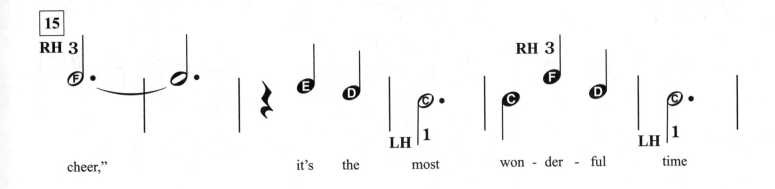

cheer," it's the most won- der - ful time

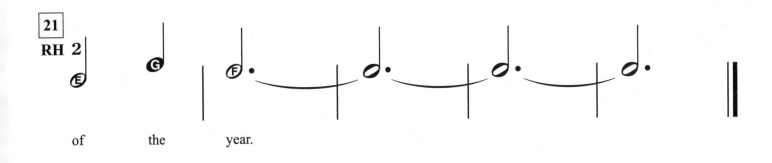

of the year.

Santa Claus Is Comin' to Town

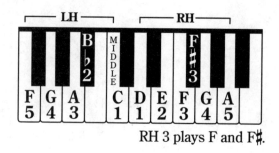

RH 3 plays F and F♯.

Words by Haven Gillespie
Music by J. Fred Coots
Arr. by Kowalchyk and Lancaster

With energy

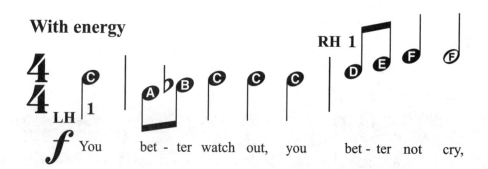
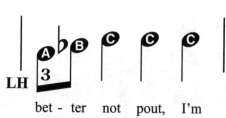

You bet-ter watch out, you bet-ter not cry, bet-ter not pout, I'm

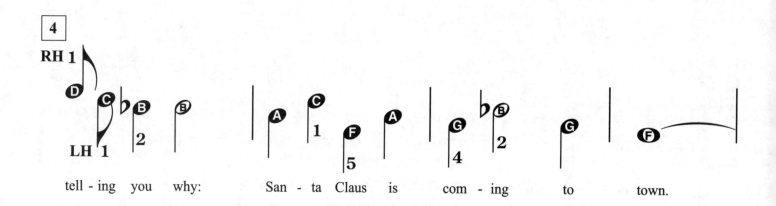

tell-ing you why: San-ta Claus is com-ing to town.

Duet Accompaniment: Student plays one octave higher.

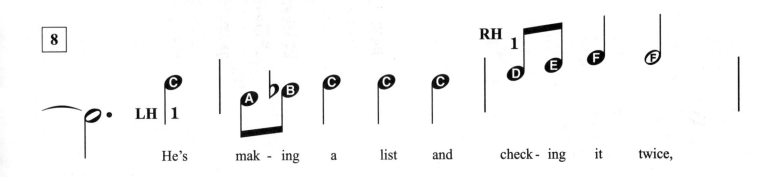

He's mak - ing a list and check - ing it twice,

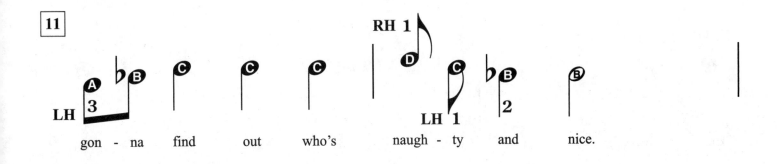

gon - na find out who's naugh - ty and nice.

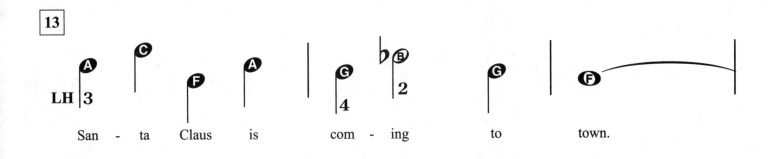

San - ta Claus is com - ing to town.

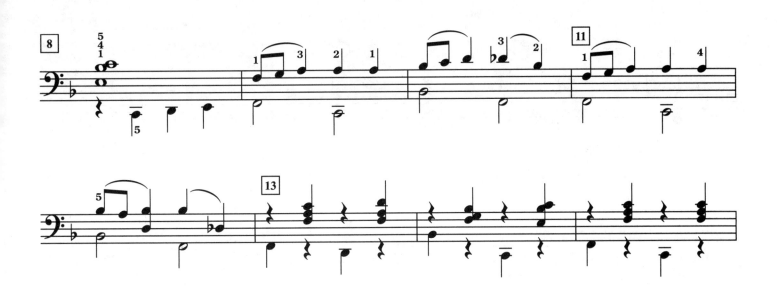

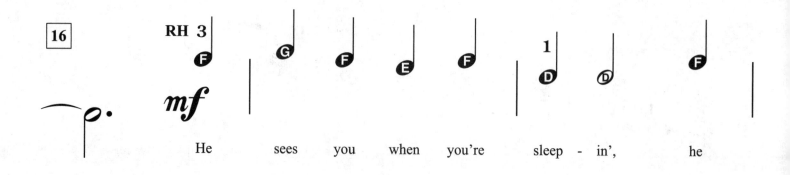

He sees you when you're sleep - in', he

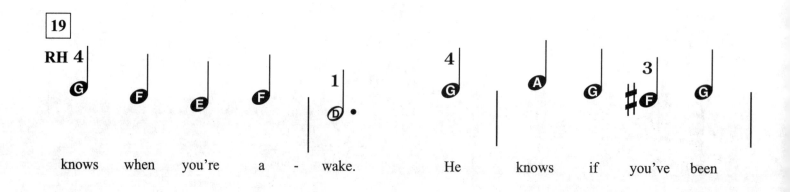

knows when you're a - wake. He knows if you've been

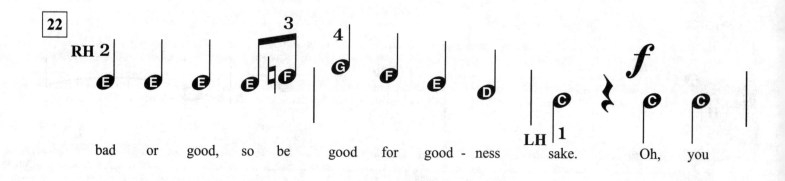

bad or good, so be good for good - ness sake. Oh, you

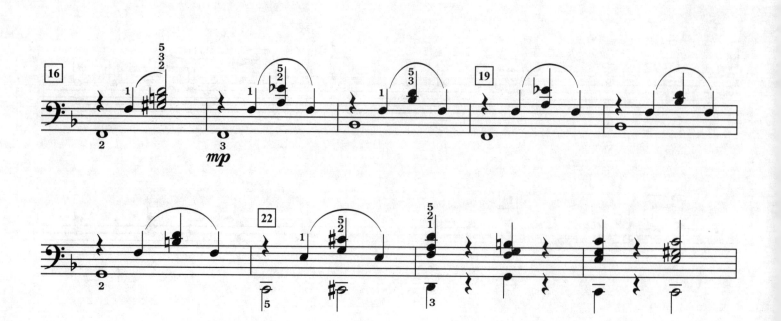

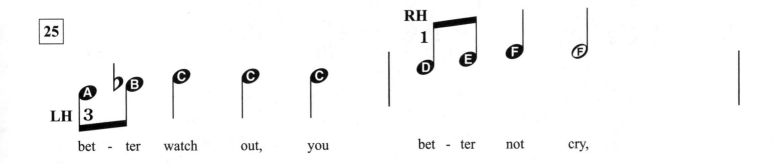

bet - ter watch out, you bet - ter not cry,

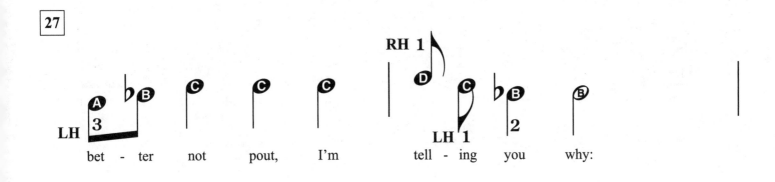

bet - ter not pout, I'm tell - ing you why:

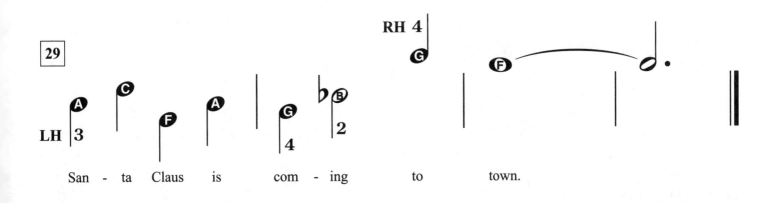

San - ta Claus is com - ing to town.

Let It Snow!
Let It Snow!
Let It Snow!

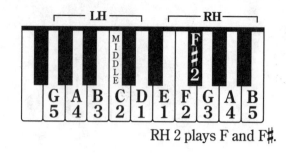

RH 2 plays F and F♯.

Words by Sammy Cahn
Music by Jule Styne
Arr. by Kowalchyk and Lancaster

Moderately fast

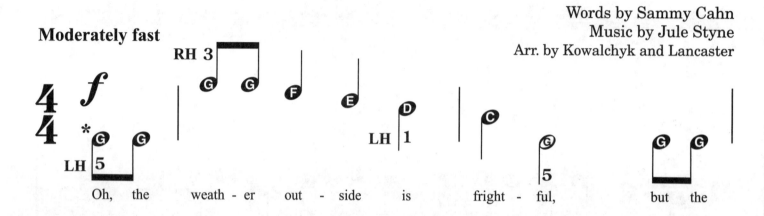

Oh, the weath-er out-side is fright-ful, but the

fire is so de-light-ful, and since we've no place to

* **Optional:** The pairs of eighth notes may be performed in swing style.

Duet Accompaniment: Student plays one octave higher.

Moderately fast

go,   let it   snow,   let it snow,   let it   snow!   It

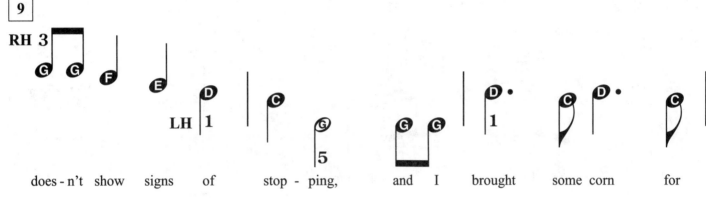

does-n't show signs of   stop - ping,   and I   brought   some corn   for

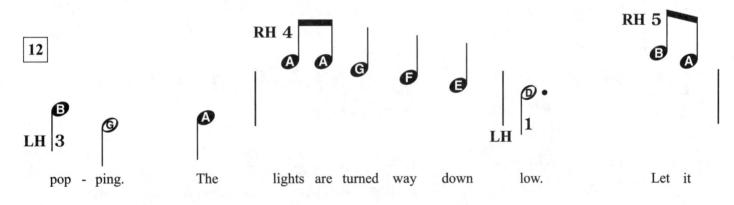

pop - ping.   The   lights are turned way   down   low.   Let it

snow, let it snow, let it snow! When we fi - nal - ly kiss good -

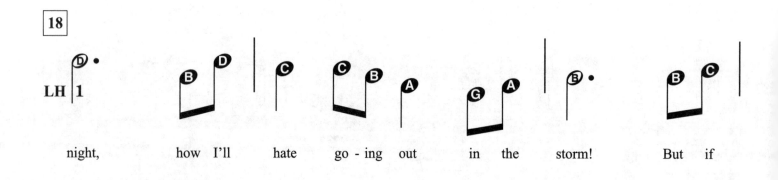

night, how I'll hate go - ing out in the storm! But if

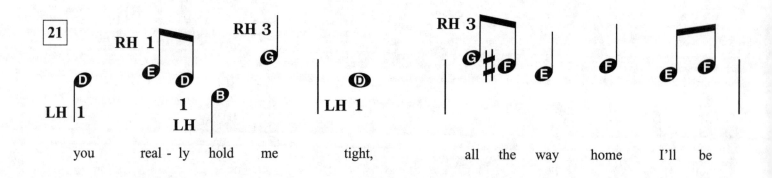

you real - ly hold me tight, all the way home I'll be